Canyon Light

The Seasons of Letchworth State Park

Printed in the United States of America by Chakra Communications, Inc.
Buffalo, New York

New York State Office of Parks, Recreation, and Historic Preservation
National Heritage for Trust

Canyon Light

The Seasons of Letchworth State Park

Photographs by Ray Minnick

Foreword by Peter G. Humphrey

First published in the United States of America in 2007
By the New York State Office of Parks, Recreation and Historic Preservation

Copyright © 2007 New York State Office of Parks, Recreation and Historic Preservation
Photographs Copyright 2007 by Ray Minnick

Printed in the United States by Chakra Communications, Inc., Buffalo, New York

ISBN 978-0-9796517-0-0

Cover Photographs by Ray Minnick
Book design, photographs and captions by Ray Minnick
Foreword by Peter G. Humphrey
Introduction/Historical Highlights by Richard Parker/Genesee State Park Region

*To the memory of my parents, who first brought me to the Genesee
Country, and set my feet on the trail that has led to the
making of these photographs. And to all those people; past,
present and future, who share my love for this timeless
treasure called Letchworth State Park.*

R.M.

Contents

FOREWORD

As a fifth generation resident of this area and the third generation of my family to serve as Chairman of the Genesee Region State Parks Commission, Letchworth State Park has come to mean a great deal to me over the years. Whether I am hiking or biking the many miles of trails, exploring the stands of old growth forest, observing it's wildlife, gazing out over scenic vistas or rafting the rapids of the Genesee River, I can't help but be amazed by this magnificent place. The sheer walls of its 600 foot deep canyon, rainbows appearing in the mist of its waterfalls, deer grazing in lawns and meadows, majestic oaks and towering hemlocks hundreds of years old, raptors soaring in the gorge; these are all sights that can never be forgotten. It reaches deep into your soul and connects with you.

William Pryor Letchworth, the man whose vision became reality, felt this connection almost 150 years ago and dedicated his life to enhancing and preserving it for future generations. Mr. Letchworth's dream was to preserve the natural beauty of the Genesee River Gorge, to create a refuge for wildlife and to preserve the woodlands and meadows that grace this river valley. He also wanted to share this wonder with the public, allowing them to be awed, inspired and thankful for nature's unique gift. I am honored to have had the opportunity to help carry on Mr. Letchworth's legacy. Ray Minnick, the photographer whose incredible images grace these pages, has also felt the "connection" all his life. Ray's daily visits with camera in hand have captured the essence of Letchworth in all it's splendor. The park's unique and spectacular geographic features along with its diverse natural resources and rich history certainly justify its standing as one of the "crown jewels" of New York State Parks. Ray's dream and mine, like Mr. Letchworth's, is to share it with the rest of the world and we believe this marvelous portfolio will do so in an enduring manner.

As you view these photographs, I hope that you will also feel connected. If this is your first exposure to Letchworth's beauty, I am quite certain that you will be drawn by it and seek to experience it first hand. For "seasoned" visitors, I am confident that the scenes depicted in this book will have you vividly recalling cherished memories. The times that I have spent at Letchworth have ensured that it will always be a special place for me and my family; I am secure in the knowledge that you will be touched by it as well.

Peter G. Humphrey

INTRODUCTION

The primary focus of this book is the natural beauty of Letchworth State Park as captured by the photographs of Ray Minnick. However, there is also a wealth of history associated with this area of the Genesee Valley and the development and preservation of the park. From the Native Americans who were the first inhabitants of this valley to the pioneers, settlers, industrial ventures and finally William Pryor Letchworth himself, there are numerous stories to be told about this land and the lives and events that shaped it. The following brief summary of historical highlights first compiled by Tom Cook, a local historian and former park interpreter, is offered with the hope and belief that readers can more fully appreciate the wonder that is Letchworth State Park by having a greater understanding of its' past.

Richard Parker, General Manager, Genesee State Park Region

Middle Fall's area showing sawmills & lattice bridge, ca. 1860

4

"Historical Highlights"
of
Letchworth State Park

LETCHWORTH STATE PARK
A Place for History and Historians

Letchworth State Park is easily one of the premier parks in the Eastern United States. The scenery and recreational facilities are outstanding and it is a historical gold mine for the researcher, historian, or anyone seeking a connection with the past of the charming Genesee Valley.

The story of Letchworth State Park is a constant stream of Native Americans, pioneers, soldiers, engineers, famous men and women and workers, flowing together in a fascinating blend of tragedies, victories, hard work and delightful stories. Although some historical episodes stand out, all aspects promise to delight the interested individual who looks for the memories.

The park was the home of the famous "White Woman of the Genesee", Mary Jemison and the great benefactor and social reformer William Pryor Letchworth. It was also the setting for the tragic Portage High Bridge, once the highest wooden bridge in the entire world, as well as the ill-fated Genesee Valley Canal whose engineering challenges were met with feats which dazzled the contemporary world. A Civil War camp and two pioneer "Ghost Towns" add to the enchantment of the memories of the park.

The visitor will be introduced to this heritage through the William Pryor Letchworth Museum with its displays, videos and interpretive staff. At the Council Grounds, where Mary Jemison is buried, stands the Seneca Council House and the Nancy Jemison Cabin. Many other historical sites in the park will help the visitor round out the story of Letchworth State Park. Whether one stays for a day or a week, they can learn and enjoy the historical episodes which have made Letchworth State Park what it is today.

The serious researcher and historian can also request arrangements to do research on Letchworth State Park and Genesee Valley history through the many historical holdings kept by the region at Letchworth State Park. All in all, Letchworth State Park has much to offer for those who delight in history — just one more thing that will make any visit to Letchworth State Park rewarding and interesting.

William Pryor Letchworth Museum

Mary Jemison & Seneca Council House

Historic Sites of Letchworth State Park

The visitor to Letchworth State Park may enjoy the fascinating heritage of the Genesee Valley and Letchworth State Park through a visit to one of the many historical sites found within the park. The most popular historical site in the park is the William Pryor Letchworth Museum which houses thousands of artifacts relating to the Genesee Valley. Special attractions in the museum include the life of Mary Jemison, the "White Woman of the Genesee", and displays describing the life of the park's benefactor, William Pryor Letchworth.

Overlooking the majestic Middle Fall, the Glen Iris Mansion was the center of Mr. Letchworth's social, business and political life until his death at the mansion in 1910. During the half century he owned the Glen Iris, it was graced by the presence of many notable people, such as Ex-President Millard Fillmore and renowned poet David Gray, many of whom planted memorial trees which still stand on the grounds of the original estate. On the bluff above the museum and the Glen Iris are the Seneca Council Grounds where the splendid statue of Mary Jemison marks the final resting-place of the famous "White Woman of the Genesee". Near the grave are other reminders of the valley's past preserved by Letchworth. They include the pre-Revolutionary War Seneca Council House where the last Iroquois Council on the Genesee was held in 1872 and the rugged log cabin of Mary Jemison's daughter, Nancy.

Glen Iris Estate 1859 - 1875

Other historical sites within the park include the iron Portage High Bridge, which replaced what was once purported to be the highest wooden railroad bridge in the world. The original wooden bridge, constructed in 1852, burned mysteriously in 1875. The massive First New York Dragoons Monument, dedicated in 1903 to the memory of the local young men who went to fight in the Civil War and returned with the dubious distinction of being the cavalry unit which lost the most men in a single engagement in the war, stands in the main park area across the river from the Parade Grounds where the units trained for battle. Two lost pioneer communities also rest within the boundaries of the park. Their demise was encouraged by the construction of the ill-fated Genesee Valley Canal whose route took it to the edge of the cliff opposite present-day Inspiration Point after an attempt to tunnel through the glacial ridge failed.

Visitors can also enjoy the graceful walks and the beautiful stone work, some of which dates back to the turn of the century. Much of this rustic work, however, was done during the 1930's by the Civilian Conservation Corps whose former camp locations are marked by stone chimneys at two locations in the park.

Stone Chimney still standing in
Gibsonville area

1st New York Dragoons Monument

Genesee Valley Canal along the
Genesee River

Land Called Seh-ga-hun-da

This land was called Seh-ga-hun-da, the "Vale of the Three Falls" by the Senecas who believed that the great beauty of Ska-ga-dee, the Middle Fall, made the sun stop at midday at the wonder of it all. It is from these people, the Senecas, that Letchworth State Park's fascinating Native American heritage comes.

The Senecas called themselves the Nun-da-wah-o, the "Great Hills People" and built their longhouse villages in the region between the Genesee River and Seneca Lake. They were a woodland people with a complex culture that based its survival on the resources of the wilderness. The beautiful valley of the Gen-nis-he-yo or Genesee River attracted them with its forest fertile soil, game and bountiful waters, so it was here they built their largest villages.

Several of these villages lay inside the present boundaries of Letchworth State Park. Deo-wes-ta was a scattered village along the neck of land, on the east side of the river near Portageville. Da-yu-it-ga-oh or Squawkie Hill was near the present site of the Mt. Morris Dam. The abandoned village of Ga-da-ho, which later came to be known as Gardeau when Mary Jemison lived there, is located in the central part of the park.

The Senecas lived for many years in the valley, secure because of their position as the "Keepers of the Western Door" of the great Iroquois League. When the American Revolution came, most of the league went on the side of the British and Washington was forced to stop the deadly frontier raids of the Senecas. In 1779 he sent five thousand men under General John Sullivan to the Genesee River with orders to destroy the lands of the Senecas. General Sullivan carried out his orders and burned many villages and fields, leaving the Indians to face the hard winter with little protection or food. The Senecas and the great league were severely weakened and fell prey to the land speculators who came to Western New York after the Revolution was over.

The Senecas sold their lands at the Big Tree Treaty in 1797 at nearby Geneseo. They didn't leave the valley right away, because they had kept reservations in the beautiful valley, two of which were located within the park. One was Squawkie Hill to the north and the other was Mary Jemison's Gardeau Reservation. By 1830, the reservations were gone and the Senecas left the land called Seh-ga-hun-da. In 1872 they returned to hold the last Council Fire on the Genesee River at the Council House, which stands on the historic Council Grounds.

But are they really gone? Today in Letchworth State Park the visitor to the museum or the Council Grounds can still hear their story and feel the presence of those who lived here long ago. At the Middle Fall they can remember the story of Mona-sha-sha, the devoted Indian wife who sacrificed herself over the fall to bring better hunting for her husband. Legend has it that her spirit returns in the form of a white deer... something occasionally seen in the park! Beautiful names such as Genesee, Deh-ga-ya-soh Creek and Gardeau still grace our maps. So maybe, just maybe, the Nun-da-wah-o have not left Seh-ga-hun-da.

Mary Jemison, "The White Woman of the Genesee"

There are few figures in American history as colorful or interesting as Mary Jemison, the famous "White Woman of the Genesee".

Around 1742 – 1743 Mary was born on a ship as her family came from Ireland to the New World. Mary spent her early life as a pioneer in the wilds of Pennsylvania. During the struggle between England and France over control of North America, she was taken captive with her family on April 5, 1758, at about age fifteen. Although her family was killed, she was adopted as Deh-ge-wa-nus, meaning "The Two Falling Voices", and spent the rest of her life with the Native Americans whom she grew to love and respect.

Mary was brought to the Genesee Valley before the Revolutionary War and lived at Little Beard's Town near present day Cuylerville, with her second husband Hiakatoo and her children. The Revolutionary War brought the Colonial Army to the Genesee Valley to destroy the villages of the Seneca. With this accomplished, in order to survive, Mary was forced to travel with her children to the Gardeau Flats where she spent the winter of 1779 with two former slaves.

When the white pioneers came to the Genesee Valley in the latter years of the 18th century, the Senecas were on reservations set aside by the provisions of the Big Tree Treaty of 1797. The treaty gave Mary her own reservation of approximately 18,000 acres of flat fertile land, forests and streams, where she lived for many years and raised her family. The years on her reservation were ones of hard work, adventure and tragedy. Although she had hoped to live out her waning years in peace surrounded by her children, she had to endure the sorrow of losing three sons, Thomas and Jesse to the hands of their brother, John, and later John himself to other Indians.

Mary journeyed to Whaley's Tavern in nearby Castile in the autumn of 1823 to talk to author James E. Seaver who had been employed to interview her and then write her life's story. The product of the work, "A Narrative of the Life of Mary Jemison" by James E. Seaver, M.D., was first printed in 1824 and has become a popular book on the "White Woman" and the world she lived in. The book has been reprinted many times and is still available at Letchworth State Park.

Mary moved to the Buffalo Creek Reservation in 1831 and lived there until her death in 1833. In 1874, when her grave was threatened due to the expansion of the city of Buffalo, NY, William Pryor Letchworth returned her to her beautiful valley where he erected a monument over her grave. In 1910 he commissioned a statue to be placed on the monument. The statue represents Mary as she came to the Genesee Valley with her oldest son Thomas on her back. Dressed in beautiful Native American clothes, it shows her not as the pioneer girl Mary Jemison, but as who she became, Deh-ge-wa-nus, the Seneca who lived on the land called Gardeau, in present day Letchworth State Park.

The Pioneer Story of Letchworth State Park

The wild lands of Letchworth State Park were, not so long ago, the frontier of a young and prosperous nation, which was moving ever westward to fulfill what has been called its "Manifest Destiny". This was the wilderness, full of dangers and adventures for the white man who came to tame it forever.

This land was the home of the Native Americans until the Big Tree Treaty in 1797 moved them to several reservations. Two of the reservations, Squawkie Hill and Gardeau (the home of Mary Jemison, the "White Woman of the Genesee") were within the boundaries of the present day park. But beyond the few Senecas living there, the lands were uninhabited.

Land speculators purchased, surveyed and sold the lands of the Genesee Valley after an ownership dispute with the state of Massachusetts was settled by the Treaty of Hartford in 1786. The buyers were hearty pioneers who surged west with the "Yankee Invasion", which started in 1790 and lasted well into the 1800's. The wilderness of the Portage Gorge kept the earliest settlers away — it wasn't until after the War of 1812 that the first settlers came. Rueben and Perry Jones are given credit as being the first settlers of the park area. In 1816 or 1817 they moved to the lands near the present day Administration Building and cleared the vast forest to build their cabins and plant their crops.

Eventually their farms prospered and they built larger, more comfortable houses. One of these now stands as the Prospect Home. Both brothers now rest along with their pioneer families in the Pioneer Cemetery near the Trout Pond in the park. Other pioneer families came into the area, people such as the Palmers, Brooks, Olcotts, Robbs, Wheelers, and Williams. They were willing to make the necessary sacrifices to build a future in a promising young land. That future centered around lumbering, milling, farming and the production of potash, which exacted a price the pioneer felt worth paying.

These pioneers began settlements — villages whose prosperity was measured by the grinding mill wheel and the swing of the sharpened axe. In the present park, at the St. Helena picnic grounds, the village of St. Helena stood in the 1800's. It was a prosperous community, which boasted two major streets, a fine bridge, twenty-five dwellings, five mills and a large inn. However, the prosperity of the villages was cut short when the Genesee Valley Canal and the railroads bypassed them. They eventually faded to the vanished ghost towns which haunt the peaceful valley today.

Even though the scars of pioneer times have been erased by the loving hand of William Pryor Letchworth and the Genesee State Park Region, the spirit and adventure of pioneer times still await the visitor to Letchworth State Park.

The Genesee Valley Canal

After the grand old Erie Canal was completed from Albany to Buffalo in 1825, the residents of the Genesee Valley began to dream. What about another canal; a man made waterway from the Erie in Rochester to the Allegany River in the South? How great progress would be if the wild Genesee could be tamed…but could it be done? The route would demand nothing less than an engineering miracle, but to the enterprising Americans of the 19th Century; engineering miracles were strong possibilities.

Work started on the new canal in 1836 and went smoothly, for the contractors could follow the gentle valley from Rochester to Mt. Morris, then south to Sonyea where they built a separate branch to feed the thriving village of Dansville. The main canal continued south through the Keshequa Valley, through Nunda, then was carried up the great Portage Hill by seventeen locks, several of which can still be seen today. At the top of the hill they dug a man-made ravine, seventy-three feet deep and two hundred and eighty-nine feet wide at the top, which is now known as the "Deep Cut". It was at this point that the engineering miracle would begin.

When the canal reached the massive cliffs across from present-day Inspiration Point, contractor Elisha Johnson decided to attempt the impossible. In order to avoid a massive point of solid rock, he proposed to build a tunnel through the high cliff. Work went well at first, but then a stop law was passed by the state and all work on the canal stopped from 1842-1848. When work was finally resumed, it was discovered that huge sections of the tunnel had caved in and more fell when attempts were made to recover the already completed work. Legend has it that many men and horses lost their lives in that ill-fated cave. It was finally decided that the tunnel couldn't be done, so instead, the ledge of the towering cliff was blasted away, which sent hundreds of tons of rock into the great Portage Gorge. As a result the canal rested on a shelf along the cliff hundreds of feet above the river, then continued south across the great slide area, which still can be seen today just below the Middle Falls.

The man-made wonder then continued south along the river to the Portageville Aqueduct where it crossed the river at a height of forty feet. From Portageville it flowed south to meet the Allegany River near Olean. The Allegany would in turn take the traveler or the goods south to the Ohio and eventually to the mighty Mississippi. When completed in 1862, the engineering marvel stretched one hundred and twenty-four miles with one hundred and six locks taking it the nearly thousand foot lift from the Erie Canal to the Allegany River.

In its heyday the Genesee Valley Canal boosted the growth of industry and agriculture along the Genesee River. Thriving canal ports developed along the route and many a tale was told of the exciting canal life and the river "canawl" gangs whose favorite pastimes were drinking and fighting. But the days of "canawling" were numbered; the state abandoned the canal in 1878 in favor of a new means of transportation… the railroad… the wonder of a new age! However, the canal had served its purpose well. Thousands of tons of forest products and manufactured goods were transported along the canal, communities boomed, industries prospered and thousands found jobs because of the canal's activities.

Today the Genesee Valley Canal is gone, but its memories still can be found in Letchworth State Park where it still stands as one of the engineering miracles of American ingenuity and where its route is now known as the Genesee Valley Canal Trail.

William Pryor Letchworth

William Pryor Letchworth is best remembered as the man who gave us beautiful Letchworth State Park, but a review of his life shows that this is only part of the story. William Pryor Letchworth was born in Brownville, Jefferson County, New York on May 26, 1823. He was the fourth child of Josiah and Ann Hance Letchworth who raised their family of eight in the village of Sherwood near Auburn, New York.

His keen intellect and dedication to work raised young Letchworth to a partnership in the Buffalo firm of Pratt and Letchworth by the age of twenty-two. The business manufactured and sold iron, saddlery, and hardware to the growing nation, and Mr. Letchworth quickly accumulated a modest fortune. Sensing there was more to the world than business, he began to travel. On one of these trips he came upon the lands he purchased in 1859 which became the Glen Iris Estate.

The magnificent estate reflects the many interests and talents of the man. As a conservationist, he restored the area to scenic splendor and created paths and walks, which served to bring the visitor closer to nature. He laid the groundwork for one of the finest arboretums in the East, while encouraging the use of scientific farming methods on the three tenant farms of the estate.

Mr. Letchworth also took interest in literature and the arts, and belonged to many societies which encouraged these arts. He himself dabbled with Victorian prose and poetry, though he signed his romantic stories with the pseudonym, Saxa Hilda. Fellow members of Buffalo's Nameless Club, such as poet David Gray and William Clement Bryant often spent pleasant days reading and writing at the Glen Iris.

A deep interest in the glen's past led Mr. Letchworth into the history and museum fields. Concentrating on the native history of the Genesee Valley, he created the Council Grounds on which he placed the famous Caneadea Council House and the Nancy Jemison Cabin. He also added the Genesee Valley Museum, which housed his extensive collection of Native American artifacts that are now part of the William Pryor Letchworth Museum. Particularly fascinated with the story of Mary Jemison, he edited several editions of her life story originally written by James Seaver. He arranged for her remains to be moved to the Council Grounds and re-interred there in a grave marked by her statue.

His interest in his fellow man blossomed after his retirement from business and he accepted an appointment to the New York State Board of Charities. For 23 years he diligently pursued the aims of The Board of Charities to foster care of unprotected children and the disadvantaged. He traveled extensively to study other states' and countries' institutions and his reports still stand as landmarks in the history of social care in this country. He was awarded a LL.D. (Doctor of Laws) for his social work, though he always felt that his greatest reward was the improved quality of life that many of the needy of society now had.

After his retirement from The Board of Charities, Mr. Letchworth devoted his final years to the creation of what would become Letchworth State Park. The state accepted his gift of approximately one thousand acres in 1907, and upon his death in 1910, Letchworth State Park was born.

Mr. Letchworth's spirit and personality live on in Letchworth State Park today. As you explore and enjoy the many facets of his park, you'll come to know and appreciate the remarkable man behind it, William Pryor Letchworth.

The Beautiful Home of a Beautiful Heart

The Glen Iris has been the center of activity and hospitality in this area since the 1860's and today it serves as a constant reminder of the life and personality of its former owner, William Pryor Letchworth.

Parts of the Greek Revival structure may have started before 1830, replacing a pioneer's log cabin, which rested upon the spot by 1820. The Palmer family sold out to developer Michael Smith, who hoped to tap the scenic beauty of the Middle Falls by opening a temperance tavern. The "Cataract House" was unsuccessful, and was up for sale by the time Mr. Letchworth had begun his search for a summer retreat.

After visiting the area in 1858, Mr. Letchworth laid plans to purchase tracts, which included the present inn and the surrounding lawns. In 1859 he purchased the 290 acre estate for $7,000.00 and with the help of landscaper William Webster, work began on what became the Glen Iris Estate.

Mr. Letchworth rejected plans to build a stately mansion on the grounds and instead developed the summer "cottage" into the Glen Iris Homestead. Over the years, as more family and friends visited Mr. Letchworth, and his charity work demanded offices and a library, he made carefully planned additions to the Glen Iris, always preserving the early lines of the house.

The Glen Iris briefly served as the park's headquarters after Mr. Letchworth's death in 1910. By 1914 it had opened as an inn with guests paying $.75 for a room and $.25 for a meal. Although the prices have changed, the warmth and hospitality have not, and today's visitors can sample both fine cuisine and glimpses of the man who made it all possible, William Pryor Letchworth.

As the poet David Gray once wrote of the Glen Iris, "And we shout and rejoice that thou art — The beautiful home of a beautiful heart". *(Voices of the Glen)*

LETCHWORTH STATE PARK MAP

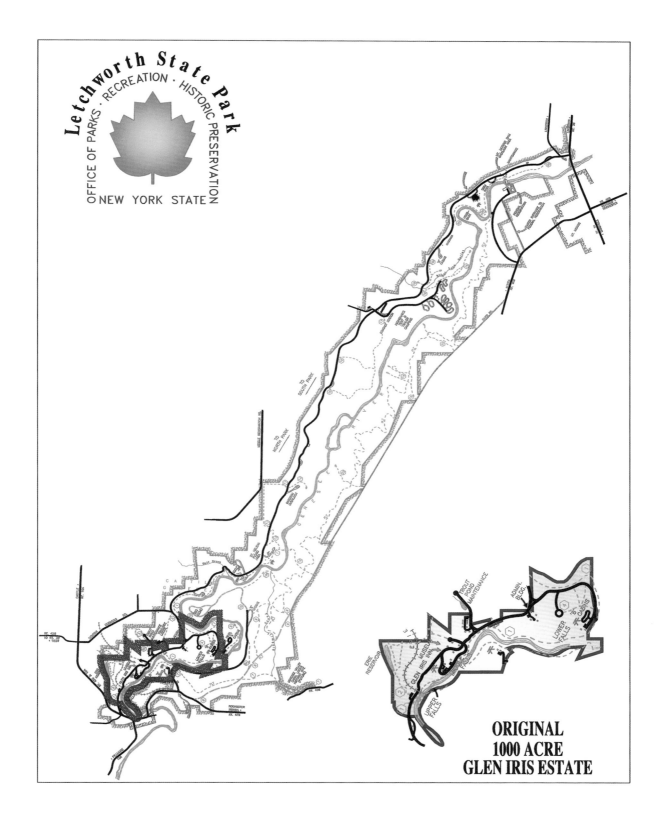

ORIGINAL
1000 ACRE
GLEN IRIS ESTATE

PHOTOGRAPHER'S PAGE

Although I am a native of Pittsburgh, Pennsylvania, it has been my good fortune to have lived the greater part of my life near Letchworth State Park, the "Grand Canyon of the East." My early interest in the outdoor world began as a boy when I accompanied my dad on hunting, fishing, and camping adventures in Pennsylvania. In later years, in New York State, I became an avid deer hunter. My photographic pursuits began by capturing on film the elusive and graceful whitetail. This first venture down the trail of nature photography naturally led to photographing the other wildlife, wildflowers, and scenic wonders that appeared daily as I have traveled the park in search of images.

I have selected the following images to share with you. They have been chosen from a collection that spans twenty years of seasons in Letchworth. These images are representative of my love of the medium of photography as well as my love of subject. They demonstrate the ever changing and almost endless variety and quality of light that illuminates the vistas in and around the canyon. If some scenes seem repetitious, please know that they are purposely included to point out these changes in light as well as the seasonal changes which alter every view.

Because of my desire to share my images of one of the most beautiful parks in the northeast, the decision was made to proceed with a book. The next determination was how best to divide it into segments that would show-case the great variety of life in the park, highlighted by the spectacular light that adds so much to the magnificent views of waterfalls, canyon, and river. The decision was relatively easy, in that the beauty of Letchworth is so well defined by the changing seasons. Watch as some images dramatically transformed by the changing colors, the angle and quality of light, and the never ending cycle of the passing and renewal of life in this 4 season paradise.

It has been said that an artist's work reflects the sum of his or her life experiences: the people he's known, the things he's seen, the music heard, the books read, the joys and sorrows of a lifetime. I believe this to be true. I would therefore, like to thank some of the people who have been involved in my photographic journey, the making of my images, and the preparation of this book. Outstanding among these would be the folks of New York State Parks, Recreation, and Historic Preservation, and notably Rich Parker, Regional Parks Manager, and his staff. A special thank you to Peter G Humphrey, who graciously consented to write the foreword. His dedication and passion for the heritage of Letchworth State Park flows from 3 generation of family involvement in park history and development. I appreciate he expertise of Doug Kern and Jeff Brown of Chakra communications, and gratefully acknowledge the generous contribution of friend and editorial consultant Mary Elena Deeney. And thanks, most of all, to a very patient and understanding wife and family who have graciously let me have time to "chase the light." They have allowed me to enjoy and photograph the rugged beauty of Letchworth State Park and the wild things that call it home.

William Pryor Letchworth, through his vision and generosity, left us a wonderful gift, and in that same spirit, I humbly make these images my gift to you. If they stir a memory, evoke an emotion, or add to your appreciation of Letchworth Park, then this book, and my challenge as a nature photographer is complete.

Join me now on a walk through the seasons of Letchworth State Park. Please share the book with your children and grandchildren, and then bring them often to this amazing and wonderful place. Be sure to bring your camera!

Ray Minnick

CANYON LIGHT
The Seasons of Letchworth State Park

"There at the place of falling waters known to the Senecas as Portage,

the carrying place for war canoes, nature touches the river with a

magic wand, and like Cinderella at the stroke of midnight, it throws off its

commonplace garb and dons robes of dazzling splendor."

~Arch Merrill
"The White Woman and Her Valley"

IMAGES OF SPRING

"Came the Spring with all its splendor, All its birds and all its blossoms,

All its flowers, leaves and grasses."

~Longfellow
"Song of Hiawatha"

Above: Looking south at Great Bend. This river scene is framed by shadbush, one of the earliest flowering shrubs in the park.
Right: The pure joy of a Spring morning at Great Bend, looking northeast at sunrise. Add birdsong and the soft echo of river rapids below.

Azalea Overlook. Wild azalea or pinxter blooms on a May morning at Great Bend. As seasons progress, the sunrise shifts north, then south as summer and autumn approach.

Canyon Mist. When conditions are right, a heavy cotton-like mist fills vast areas of the gorge. From a distance, this appears as a hovering band of white following the winding river.

*"Every day is a renewal,
every morning the daily miracle.
The joy you feel is life."*

~Gertrude Stein

Above and Left: Beautiful morning light occurs at and just before sunrise, often following the passage of storm systems.

This iron bridge, an engineering marvel in itself, replaced the original wooden span. William Pryor Letchworth had his first view of the Portage Falls from here in 1858.

Silent footsteps. This beautifully crafted stone stairway lies hidden in the forest above Glen Iris. How old is it, and who walked these steps to view the falls of the Genesee?

Above left: A lone yellow violet blooms along Trail 6 on the east side of the gorge.
Above right: Hepaticas can be found in April among fallen oak leaves.
Below: Dame's rocket drifts in this locust grove near the Perry entrance to the park.

"A few days ago, not a bird, not a sound; everything rigid and severe; then, in a day the barriers of winter give way, and spring comes like an inundation. In a twinkling all is changed."

~John Burroughs

Above: Pink lady's slipper or moccasin flower. Becoming harder to find, this colorful spring bloom is a member of the orchid family. Below: A week old whitetail fawn. odorless and colored for protection, spends its day hidden from predators.

Seh-ga-hun-da (Seneca) Vale of Three Falls.
"Here the sun stands still, and gleaming radiance crowns the Genesee."

~Carleton Burke

28

Het-ga-oh (Waters rush like the wind).
Beneath the towering railroad bridge, the power of the Upper Falls creates a constant swirling mist as new spring growth follows the icy grip of winter on this wet cliffside.

In Seneca Legend, the Middle Falls stood out with such beauty at noonday that the sun would pause for a moment above it in passing. It is the home of the "jungies", underwater spirits.

The Lower Falls or Gah-nee-gah-tah, is the home of more little people who beat magic drums, opening the day, and turning flowers toward the light.

*"Rain drifts forever in this place, tossed from the waterfall's long white lace,
And goldenrod and rose-root shake, In wind that they forever make."*

~Andrew Young

A stand of mayapple covers this hillside above the William Pryor Letchworth museum. The single fruit of this plant was used in earlier times to make mayapple jelly.
Previous page at bottom: Wildflowers at the Middle Falls.

A splash of yellow color decorates this small brook near the Middle Falls. The edible greens of this early spring plant are called "cowslips".

To The Memory of Mary Jemison

Whose home during more than seventy years of a life of strange
vicissitude was among the Senecas upon the banks of this river;
and whose history, inseparably connected with that
of this valley,has caused her to be known as
"The white woman of the Genesee"

Gardeau Flats.
Here the Genesee winds gently northward toward Smokey Hollow and the Highbanks. For fifty years this was home to Mary Jemison, "the white woman", and her family. From that time until the 1950's, these fertile lands were actively farmed. Today this is one of the most wild and remote areas of the park, and is home to the whitetail, otter, beaver, and eagle.

Canyon wall at Deh-ga-ya-soh.
In front of present day Pinewood Lodge, a pink misty light bounces off rock walls and ledges.

A male baltimore oriole rests after its arrival in May. Their northward migration follows the increase in insect life on which they feed.

East-facing sand hills in the park are favorite den locations for the red fox. This pup, one of 5 in a litter, awaits the return of its parents with food.

*"you must not know too much,
or be too precise or scientific about
birds and trees and flowers.
A certain free margin… helps your
enjoyment of these things."*

~Walt Whitman

38

A great horned owl chick on its first day out of the nest. Our largest owl, these fierce predators begin nesting in the bitter cold of February so that their young will be hatched and fed in the Spring, a season of plenty in Letchworth Park.
Opposite page top: New York's State bird, the eastern bluebird, works tirelessly to feed young.
Left: Great blue herons raise their young in a rookery near Lee's Landing.
Right: A fledgling robin has tumbled from its nest, and will be fed by parent birds until able to take care of itself.

Colors of Springtime. In the 1930's, the Civilian Conservation Corps had 4 camps in operation at Letchworth Park. Most of the existing roads, bridges, stone walls and stairs were built by these hard working young men. A statue dedicated to their lasting contribution can be seen near the south swim pool.

IMAGES OF SUMMER

"Bright Summer Dream

of white cascade

of lake, and wood, and river!

The vision from the eye may fade,

The heart keeps it forever."

~James Johnston

Flowing Through Time.
Pink light on the Genesee River at Great Bend.

*"These are true mornings of Creation, original
and poetic days, not mere reflections of the past.
There is no lingering of yesterday fogs, only
such a mist as might have adorned the first morning."*

~Henry David Thoreau

Left: An area of dense shrubbery is the favorite nesting territory of the northern cardinal.

Below: A monarch butterfly feeds on the nectar of swamp milkweed.

Right: Windblown seeds of common milkweed decorate New England asters.

Below right: A dew-laden web, with goldenrod and New England asters.

The softly muted colors of a misty dawn await the warming rays of the sun.
Above: A doe in silhouette.
Below: Archery field oaks.

Storm light imparts a somber tone to the canyon views.
Above: A solitary beam of sunlight contrasts with a menacing storm sky over Great Bend.
Below: Ominous rain clouds hover low over Inspiration Point.

"Like us, rivers spring from obscure sources and flow toward unavoidable destinations. If the sea represents eternity, the rivers that flow into them are the twisting, bold, and unstoppable currents of time."

~Jerry Dennis

The latent power of the Genesee is evidenced by these rocks deposited in mid-stream below the Upper Falls.

Opposite page, above: The Lower Falls and riverbed above the footbridge.

Opposite page, below: The Middle Falls in summer as viewed from Glen Iris.

Rainbow at the Upper Falls.
The intensity of color in this rainbow is determined by the direction of the sun's rays, and the amount of spray and mist in the air.

A dome of high clouds and a colorful sunrise have combined to create this compelling river scene above the Middle Falls.

Twin fawns in a meadow enjoy the bounty of summer. A grey, heavier layer of winter hair will soon replace their spotted coats.

A whitetail doe and fawn. Fawns often remain with their mother into the second year.

During the long days of summer, Whitetail bucks feed and rest in preparation for the fall rut. It is common to see several bucks together at this time, as they grow new antlers and establish a pecking order of dominance.

A two year old buck in velvet pauses on the way to its bedding area.

*"Man is not himself only… he is all that he sees;
all that flows from him from a thousand sources…
he is the land, the lift of its mountain lines,
the reach of its valleys."*

~Mary Austin

Above: Depending on atmospheric conditions, the colors of a Letchworth Park sunrise can be as subtle or as dramatic as an artist's palette.
Left: A seasonal parade of wildflowers complements the scenic grandeur of Letchworth. Trillium, columbine, wild rose and daisies are but a few.

Morning light finds its way into this red pine plantation along the Mary Jemison Trail. Foxglove, ferns, and striped maple thrive in the understory.

The northern maidenhair fern is a beautiful example of nature's perfection in pattern and symmetry. It prefers moist and shaded slopes such as those found along the East Park Road.

"Like a great poet, nature is capable of producing the most stunning effects with the smallest means."
~Heine

Clockwise from top left: Orange hawkweed, wild rose (New York's state flower), orange mycena mushroom, golden garden spider.

Yellow Iris bloom along a peaceful bend in the river above Lee's Landing. The landing was so called because it offered a rare fording place along the river bottom.

The white deer embodies the true spirit of Letchworth Park lore and legend. Whether a true albino, or a piebald like this one, a white deer always attracts interest and attention.

IMAGES OF AUTUMN

"In the forest, fall is the season of light-

filling the woodlands with a luminous radiance

unknown at other seasons of the year."

~Edwin Way Teale

The ever-changing panorama from Inspiration Point.
Late afternoon October sunlight slants through the mist at the Middle Falls.
Previous page: An October afternoon at the Upper Falls.

Clearing blue sky and golden beech leaves add color to this fog-shrouded grove of birches.

"How beautifully the leaves grow old. How full of light and color are their last days."

~John Burroughs

This page: Pine Pond reflections.

Opposite page: The Middle Falls from Glen Iris.

Deh-ga-ya-soh Creek empties into the Genesee under the arch bridge at the bottom of Eagle Hill. This view is from Trail 7 on the east side of the park.

Above: The beaver pond on the East Park Road provides habitat for a variety of wildlife including beaver, river otter, mink and muskrats. Reptiles and amphibians of many species abound.
Below: The canada goose is one of many birds to be seen at the beaver pond. Migrating ducks, great blue heron, bittern, and many songbirds may be observed here.

The Lower Falls from Sugarloaf.

"God wrought for us this scene beyond compare,
But one man's loving hand protected it,
And gave it to his fellow men to share."

~Sarah Evans Letchworth
Inscribed on a plaque at Inspiration Point

Two views of historic Wolf Creek. Whaley's sawmill near the mouth of the creek was one of the earliest industries in the area, and was reached by the old Wolf Creek Road from Castile Village.

Above: The hog's-back is a unique geological formation at the north end of the park, just upstream from the Mount Morris Dam.
Below: Sunrise over Inspiration Point.

Most of the area of present day Letchworth Park was once a patchwork of small farms. This old wooden gate serves as a reminder of this past way of life.
Opposite page: Letchworth leaf studies.

"This is the end of blossom, berry, leaf;
This is the end of the velvet antlered day."

~Carleton Burke

On a typical November morning, with wet snow flurries in the air, a whitetail buck cruises the Genesee River bottoms in search of does.

Left: Lee's Landing, on the Genesee, where a quiet backwater reflects autumn's colorful display.

Below: The Wolf Creek escarpment and the blue haze of an October afternoon.

Leaf strewn Trail 7, which crosses the East Park Road, is a walk along the route of the Genesee Valley Canal.

The west wall of the gorge at Great Bend as seen from Humphrey's Point.

A few oak leaves cling stubbornly as an old giant awaits the approach of yet another winter.

IMAGES OF WINTER

"...And it obscures the sky and fills the

vistas of the woods."

~John Burroughs

Pale winter sunlight falls upon new snow at the canyon's edge.
Previous page: A fresh snowfall, broken only by the tracks of deer searching for food.

Winter's first snowfall on fall color along a park trail.

A section of Gorge Trail.

Along the Gorge Trail between Inspiration Point and the Lower Falls.

A stark winter view of the Upper and Middle Falls from Inspiration Point.

"Every day a new picture is painted and framed."

~Henry David Thoreau

Right and below: An ice storm leaves a glittering coat of ice on every tree and rock surface.

Clockwise from top left: Male northern cardinal, bluejay, chipping sparrow, chickadee.

Many species of birds make their winter home in Letchworth State Park. Over-wintering bluebirds and robins can occasionally be found in sheltered areas with a food supply.
Above: Northern cardinal female.

At the upper falls, constantly rising mist freezes on each branch, twig and blade of grass. On sunny winter days, a rainbow may color this wonderland of crystals.

"A clear, cold morning, one of those icy-brittle mornings when sounds carry far."

~Hal Borland

Right: The cycle of water freezing, expanding and breaking away rock is part of the on-going process of eroding away the canyon walls.

Below: The Upper Falls and the Genesee in the icy grip of winter.

Shadow Pool awaits the return of spring. In other seasons, it is a quiet place of peaceful reflections.

Ice-coated branches at the Glen Iris fountain pool.

Left: Snow sparkles in the crisp, clear morning light at the Archery Field Overlook.

Below: Lamplight and a drifted fence at Inspiration Point.

The branches of pine, hemlock, and beech are laden with fresh snow along the trail to the Lower Falls.

Left: In times of deep snow, deer are forced to dig for leaves, grass and acorns.

Below: In late winter, deer conserve energy and body heat by moving as little as possible between feeding and bedding areas.

Whitetail bucks in winter. Above: A cold weather front and fresh snowfall may create an increase in deer activity.
Below: 3 months of intense rut activity, followed by the stress of a hard winter, can tax the energy reserves of whitetail bucks.

Some colors of winter.
If we look closely, some cheerful color can be found even in the cold, grey days of winter. Maple leaves, dogwood berries, and raspberry accent their snowbound environment.

Trout pond in winter.

A winter dawn in the southeastern sky over Great Bend.

In the north canyon, snow and a layer of ice on the river reflect the colors of sunrise.

"You may roam the wide world over,
Far back of beyond you may go;
Someday you'll come back,
To follow the track,
Of the Whitetail deer in the snow."

~author unknown